Stories Worthy of Passing On

Stories Worthy of Passing On

Joyce Payne Clayton

Illustrated by Jan Strock

Ivy House
Publishing Group

www.ivyhousebooks.com

Cover art:
From a painting © United Methodist Publishing House.
Used by permission.

All scripture quotations, unless otherwise noted, are from the
New Revised Standard Version of the Holy Bible.
Copyright 1989, Division of Christian Education Council of
the Churches of Christ in the U.S.A.

PUBLISHED BY IVY HOUSE PUBLISHING GROUP
5122 Bur Oak Circle, Raleigh, NC 27612
United States of America
919-782-0281

ISBN: 1-57197-340-0
Library of Congress Control Number: 2002113070

Copyright © 2003 Joyce Payne Clayton
All rights reserved, which includes the right to reproduce this book or portions thereof in any form
whatsoever except as provided by the U.S. Copyright Law.
Printed in China

Dedicated to my grandchildren:

Jessica Clayton
Dustin Clayton
Darty Clayton
David Clayton
Dana Clayton

Psalms 78:5-7

He established a decree in Jacob, and appointed a law in Israel, which he commanded our ancestors to teach their children; that the next generation might know Him, the children yet unborn, and rise up and tell them to their children, so that they should set their hope in God, and not forget the works of God, but keep His commandments.

Foreword

All of us have stories about favorite teachers, stories that we enjoy remembering and sharing with others. Great teachers rein us in, set us aright, and send us on our way again. I believe great teachers are inspired; they are not motivated by money or acclaim. Their inspiration is born of an innate faith, an optimism, an unshakable belief that the march of time brings more good than ill. This inspiration is at the root of whatever subject is being taught. One of my favorite teachers taught French, and though I have forgotten most of the French I learned in that class, the more important lessons I learned from that teacher changed me forever, lessons I will never forget, lessons in life.

The simple parables in *Stories Worthy of Passing On* are the work of an inspired teacher. Upon such everyday objects as a box of crayons, a balloon, children's building blocks, or a blackberry vine, stories are woven. One imagines the eager child faces, perceiving in an object as familiar to them as a crayon, something new—something unexpected—a metaphor or symbol that uplifts and expands their impressionable minds, helping them comprehend lessons in life and the teachings of the Bible.

Many of the stories fill me with emotion. As I read them I recall similar lessons I heard in Sunday school as a small boy, those now juxtaposed with the lessons learned in "life's hard school," as the poet John Greenleaf Whittier called it. Indeed, many of the stories are very nearly poetic, not surprising considering the author's love of poetry. I have known Joyce Clayton for forty years. She is the personification of the spirit that infuses her stories—enthusiasm, idealism, patience, diligence, hope, love of life, and strong faith in God.

John May
May 15, 2002

Acknowledgments

A special thank you to:
Jesus Christ to whom all honor, glory, and praise belongs.
Those who encouraged me.
All the children who eagerly listened.

For Parents and Teachers

For forty years I have been a Sunday School teacher of four- to ten-year-old children. Throughout my experience I have learned more from children than I have probably taught. Children are so innocent and eager to learn and they express their opinions quickly. You have to be ready to answer any and all questions in some manner or fashion.

I learned that there is a great need for children to grow up knowing who God really is and that He loves them unconditionally. If this love is instilled into the life of every child, he or she will be equipped to face life without fear. The knowledge of God helps them build character based upon His laws.

Teaching has really been a challenge in my life because I have to stay alert to all opportunities given to me by God. As the Scriptures are read, the lessons are learned, and they need to be passed on. God speaks to every generation through His Word; we only have to be open and listen for His guidance.

These short sermon stories are taught with objects, pictures and examples. The stories, based on Scripture, need to be told to future generations. Children tend to remember easily if they are shown examples. Remember, younger children have short attention spans, so keep it brief, simple and to the point.

As this book is read, I pray the love of God will be instilled into the life of every child who hears one of these stories. These stories are to be told or read to children to provide them an opportunity to hear and respond to God's love.

Abundance

How many of you have a birdhouse in your yard? What kinds of birds live in those houses? I like to watch birds feeding in the yard. I have a bird feeder outside that I can see from my window.

One day the birds were eating, but most of them were under the feeder on the ground. They were scratching around on the ground looking for seeds that were knocked out of the bird feeder by other birds. Only one or two birds were in the feeder itself.

The birds were only interested in the seeds that had fallen from above. If only they had looked up they would not have had to scratch around on the ground for food. The bird feeder was full of seeds. They did not know what they were missing.

Sometimes we miss out on the better things in life because we do not look up to Jesus. He said that He came to give us a more abundant life. We just fail to follow His teachings sometimes.

Learn more about His teachings by reading the Bible more and praying more.

John 10:10
"The thief comes to steal and destroy; I came that they may have life, and have it more abundantly."

Accountability

These one dollar bills are for you. Each one of you may take one. There is one thing you have to do to get one of these bills. You have to promise that you will use it for good.

The Bible tells a story of a rich man who hired an accountant to handle his money. Someone reported to the rich man that his accountant was dishonest. The rich ruler called the accountant and told him to account for himself.

The accountant went to each of the ruler's debtors and wrote new contracts for less than the original one. Some of the bills were cut in half. The accountant told the ruler it was better to collect half than not collect any money at all.

We will be held accountable for how we handle our money. If we are not honest with small amounts of money, then we can't be trusted with large amounts.

Remember that you have to answer to God about how you use your money. I will ask you next week what you did with your one dollar. Let it be a good report.

Luke 16:10
"Whoever is faithful in a very little is faithful also in much; and whoever is dishonest in a very little is dishonest also in much."

Anchor

Boy, this is really heavy. I can hardly lift it. I wouldn't like to drop it on my foot. This long chain hooked to it is also heavy. Do you know what it is? Yes, it is an anchor for a boat.

When we go fishing we drop the anchor into the water to hold the boat steady while we fish. The anchor digs into the soil and holds until we pull it up. It makes a person feel safe and secure and lets them know that they will not drift off in the wrong direction. Anchor means "to be firmly fixed in any way."

We can anchor our beliefs in things and people. Hope also is an anchor of the soul. The Bible tells us to let Jesus be our anchor. Our faith and trust should be put in Him. He is the one to hold us secure and keep us on the correct path. When the storms of life come, His anchor holds fast and will not give way.

Remember this the next time you are in a boat and an anchor is thrown out.

Hebrews 6:19
We have this hope, a sure and steadfast anchor of the soul, a hope that enters the inner shrine behind the curtain.

Balloons

Here are two balloons with air inside. They look exactly alike. They are both blue and they are the same size. Both have separate strings attached to them and are filled with gases. Can you see any other differences in the two balloons? No? I can't either, but watch what happens when I let go of them. One balloon sinks to the floor and one balloon floats to the ceiling.

What do you think caused this? Well, the balloons had different gases on the inside. The one that fell to the floor had oxygen on the inside, and the one that rose to the ceiling had helium on the inside. Helium is much lighter than oxygen, therefore it goes up. Often, what is on the inside makes a difference how something or someone acts.

Jesus taught this to His disciples. Jesus said a man thinks what is in his heart. What we have inside our hearts makes a in difference how we act.

Decide to let your actions reflect the goodness in your heart.

Luke 6:45
"The good man out of the goodness of the good treasures of his heart produces good, and the evil man out of his evil treasures produces evil; for it's out of the abundance of the heart the mouth speaks."

Beach Sand

A little girl was building a sandcastle on the beach. She had really worked hard for several hours. With her back to the ocean, an unexpected wave came, and guess what happened? I'm sure you know if you have ever built a sandcastle on the beach. In just a few seconds the castle was washed away. The beach looked clean and smooth as the water went back into the ocean.

I have a bucket full of water and a box with a pile of sand in it. Watch what happens as I pour the water over the sand. It flattens out smooth.

When I look at how clean and smooth the sand is after the water washes over it, I think about how Jesus takes our sin away and makes us clean. Just as the ocean cleans the beach, Jesus takes our sins away, never to be remembered. God made this possible by letting Jesus die on the cross for our sins.

The next time you see sand on the beach being washed away, think about what Jesus did for you.

Revelation 1:5
And from Jesus Christ, the faithful witness, the firstborn of the dead, and ruler of the kings of the earth. To him who loves us and freed us from our sins by his blood.

Beans and Biscuits

Once there was a man in a foreign country who longed to come to the United States. He heard there were lots of opportunities and work here. He had no money for the boat ticket.

He worked very hard for years, saving his money. Finally, he had enough money for the ticket and had two dollars left.

He packed his belongings and enough beans and biscuits to last the entire trip. Every day for breakfast, lunch, and dinner he had cold canned beans and biscuits. By the fourth day he was so tired of eating beans and biscuits, the thought of them almost made him sick. Can you imagine eating the same thing three times a day for four days in a row?

One day he was walking on the deck and smelled food. He followed the smell and came to a cafeteria. He only had two dollars but the food smelled so good to him. He asked, "How much would a meal cost?" The lady answered, "If you bought a ticket for the boat trip, all of the meals are free."

So you see, all of his meals had already been paid for. He only had to accept the free food.

The Bible says our ticket to heaven has already been paid for. Jesus paid for it by dying on the cross for our sins. What a wonderful God!

Check out the Bible and see exactly what our ticket provides for us.

John 3:16
For God so loved the world that he gave his only Son, so that everyone who believes in him may not perish but have eternal life.

Big Eraser

When I was a child, I was disciplined by my parents many times. I remember one time that I disobeyed my parents and went where I should not have gone. My parents were waiting anxiously for my return. I knew I would be punished for disobeying. I came in the door shaking and ashamed, expecting punishment.

My parents had heard about a car accident and thought that I might have been involved. They were so relieved to see that I was okay, that they had erased all thoughts of punishment.

God has a big eraser also. The parables of the lost coin and the lost sheep tell us this. Upon finding the lost coin and the lost sheep, their owners were not angry. They were joyful that their property had been found.

When we are sorry for doing wrong, God welcomes our return.

Remember, your parents love you and so does God.

Luke 15:10
"Just so, I tell you, there is joy in the presence of the angels of God over one sinner who repents."

Boomerang

Do you know what this is? The painting on it tells stories passed down from generation to generation. It is a boomerang made by the Aborigines of Australia. Our Bible came about by writing down stories that had also been passed down over many years.

The Aborigines use a boomerang to teach their children about their past. They throw it a certain way and it returns to them. They taught their children that when they gave love, it would return to them.

Jesus, in His teachings, taught the same thing. Jesus gave us a commandment to love one another. The measure we give will be given back to us.

There are many ways we can show kindness. Let's see if we can name some.

- Visit a sick friend.
- Send a card.
- Do a chore for someone.
- Give smiles.
- In other words, show love in all that you do.

Remember to show love by being kind to others.

Luke 6:38
"Give and it will be given to you. A good measure, pressed down, shaken together, running over, will be put into your lap; for the measure you give will be the measure you get back."

Boy Jesus

When Jesus was twelve years old, He went with His parents to Jerusalem to celebrate the feast of the Passover. On the return trip home, his parents realized Jesus was not among the crowd. His parents returned to Jerusalem to find Him sitting in the Temple. Jesus was asking the priests questions and answering questions that the priests asked Him. Jesus told his parents that He was going about His Father's business.

No stories were recorded about Jesus after He went to the Temple until He was about thirty years old. The Bible says that He grew in wisdom and stature.

What did He do and learn in eighteen years? The Bible doesn't say, but we can tell what a person did or learned by the way they act when they are older. According to the Bible, Jesus learned Scriptures. He learned how to resist temptation, and to be kind, humble, and forgiving. He learned to be obedient to His Father's Word.

Learn to be like Jesus by following Jesus and setting examples.

Luke 2:52
And Jesus increased in wisdom and in years, and in divine and human favor.

Can of Milk

Watch as I put a hole in the top of this can of milk. Now try to pour the milk from the can. The milk doesn't come out very freely. What do you suppose would make the milk come out freely? I'm sure it would come out freely if I took the whole top off, but that is not necessary. I only have to punch one more hole in the top to let the milk come out freely. The second hole lets air go inside the can to push the milk out.

We can compare ourselves to this can of milk. We are full of God's blessings and we need to pour them onto someone else. We need help to love some people.

If we let The Holy Spirit into our hearts we can accomplish the work God has for us to do. God gave us The Holy Spirit after He ascended into heaven. We need The Holy Spirit to help us let the good things flow from our lives freely.

Ask The Holy Spirit to come into your heart.

John 14:26
"But the advocate, The Holy Spirit, whom the Father will send in my name, will teach you everything, and remind you of all I have said to you."

Cornerstones

What do you think these cement blocks were made for? "To build something" is the correct answer. It takes lots of these to build a house or a building. The cornerstones are the most important because they hold up the rest of the building.

The Bible says we are to become living building stones for God to use to help build His church. The church is made up of people. Jesus is the cornerstone of the church. He will always hold us up and never disappoint those who put their trust in Him. Jesus is the most honored and important part of the church. The church was founded upon Him.

Whenever you see a building going up, remember to let Jesus be your cornerstone.

1 Peter 2:6
For it stands in scripture: "See, I am laying in Zion a stone, a cornerstone chosen and precious; and whoever believes in him will not be put to shame."

Crayons

What color is your favorite crayon? Red, blue, purple, pink, yellow; all of these are pretty, bright colors. My husband likes black and gray. So, you see, different people prefer different colors.

Some crayons are dull in their color; some even have weird names like magenta. Some crayons are sharp and some are dull. Some are short and some are long. Some are pretty and I even think some of them are ugly. They are all different colors . . . but live in the same box.

Let's look at this box of crayons and compare them to people. We can learn a lot from a box of crayons. There are dull people, bright people, people with weird names, short people, and all different colors of people. So, we are a lot like a box of crayons.

Jesus teaches us that we should learn to live together in love, although we are different in a lot of ways. The more we learn about Jesus, the more we can become like Him.

Learn about Jesus by reading the Bible and going to church.

John 15:12
"This is my commandment, that you love one another as I have loved you."

Crumbs

What are these I have scattered all over the floor? Would you like to eat these now? Of course not; they are crumbs that have been swept from the floor under the table. Crumbs usually go to the dogs or cats, maybe with some other scraps.

Jesus was talking to a woman from Cana. She told Jesus she wasn't worthy to pick up the crumbs from under His table. What did she mean by this? Do you know what "worthy" means? It means "deserving, good, or important enough." The woman from Cana thought she was not deserving or good enough.

Jesus showed us how important we are to Him. He died on the cross for our sins so that we could have eternal life with Him. Everyone who believes He did this for us has eternal life.

The next time you drop crumbs on the floor, remember how important you are to God.

Matthew 15:27
She said, "Yes, Lord, yet even the dogs eat the crumbs that fall from their masters' table."

Cups

I have here a cup that is dirty on the outside but clean on the inside. Here is another cup that is clean on the outside but dirty on the inside. Which cup would you rather drink from? The one that is clean on the inside would be a better choice. It is more important to keep the cup clean on the inside than on the outside.

Which is more important to keep clean, our hearts or our hands? It is more important to keep the heart clean—but it doesn't mean that we are not to wash our hands.

Jesus told the Pharisees to first clean the inside of themselves, and then their whole selves would be clean. The Pharisees were very strict in keeping the laws of their own religion. Their hearts were not clean because they were full of hate and greed. How do we get our hearts clean? Jesus can clean our hearts by forgiving our sins. We can say, "Create in me a clean heart," and He is eager to forgive.

Repeat this prayer, "Dear Jesus, take the sin from my heart and make me clean."

Matthew 23:25–26

"Woe to you, Scribes and Pharisees, hypocrites! For you clean the outside of the cup and of the plate, but inside they are full of greed and self-indulgence. You blind Pharisee! First clean the inside of the cup so that the outside also may become clean."

David and Goliath

Here are five smooth stones. Can you guess where they came from? They came from the brook in Israel where David killed Goliath the giant.

The Israelites were slaves of the Philistines. In the Philistine army there was a giant by the name of Goliath. All the Israelite soldiers were afraid of him and would not fight him. The Israelites needed someone to beat this giant, then the Philistines would become slaves to the Israelites.

There was a young shepherd by the name of David who was sent to take food to his brothers in the battlefield. David found out about Goliath and offered to fight the giant. Everyone laughed at him because he was only a boy. David knew that God would be with him and he wasn't afraid.

David took his slingshot and five small stones from a brook to confront Goliath. David ran toward the giant. He put a stone in his sling and struck Goliath in the center of his forehead. That one stone killed Goliath.

The Israelites cheered because they were free. The Philistines fled after they saw Goliath was dead. David had trusted God to do this great thing.

When you are in trouble, remember, with God's help, even the smallest person can make a difference.

1 Samuel 17:50
So David prevailed over the Philistines with a sling and a stone, striking down the Philistine and killing him; there was no sword in David's hand.

Direction

Look at the five cards and the beanbag on the table. Now play the game. What do you mean, you don't have directions? A game is hard to play without directions. Everyone would be trying to play a different way, making up their own rules.

Here are the rules. Each card is numbered. The floor is marked off in five numbered spaces. Draw a card. With your beanbag, try to hit the space on the floor that has the same number as your card.

As you can see, it is much easier to play a game when you have directions. It makes the game complete.

Life is the same way; without directions it can be very difficult. After the crucifixion and resurrection, the disciples didn't know what to do. Without Jesus as their leader, they had no direction.

They had been fishing all day and had caught nothing. Jesus appeared to them and gave them directions about where to cast their nets. Their nets were overflowing with fish after listening to Jesus' directions.

We need to listen to Jesus' directions for our lives. Many directions are given to us in the Bible. God gives us directions through Jesus.

Read, listen and pray.

John 21:6
He said to them, "Cast the net to the right side of the boat, and you will find some." So they cast it, and now they were not able to haul it in because there were so many fish.

Dividing Line

You promised earlier that you would do something good with the money given to you. What did you do with your dollar? Dana put hers in the collection plate. Hannah gave hers to food relief. Those were good things to do. If you did not do something good with your dollar, you are now being held accountable.

Those of you who did good things with your money, step to the right of the tape line on the floor. Those who did selfish things, step to the left of the line.

Jesus told the story of a rich man who had a beggar at his gate. The rich man did nothing to help the beggar. The beggar died and went to heaven to be with Abraham and Moses. The rich man died and went to live in torment. One day, from far away, the rich man saw Abraham and the beggar. The rich man begged for water, but the beggar could not give any to him because he could not go past the dividing line that separated good from evil. The rich man then asked Abraham to send the beggar to his brothers and warn them about the terrible place.

Father Abraham told him his brothers had Scriptures, and that if they didn't believe Moses and the prophets, they would not believe anyone else, even if they were risen from the dead.

Like the rich man, you will be held accountable for the things you do, so remember to do good while you can.

Luke 16:25

But Abraham said, "Child, remember that during your lifetime you received your good things, and Lazarus in the like manner evil things; but now he is comforted here, and you are in agony."

Earth

Let's find the United States on this large globe of the earth. It is a very tiny place compared to the rest of the world. About three-fourths of the earth looks like water and about one-fourth looks like land.

The Bible tells us that God formed the earth out of nothing. If I said, "Let's make a birdhouse," we would need wood, nails, a hammer, and a saw. God could build with nothing in His hand. He made the world and put us into it. He wanted someone He could talk with and be friends with.

If we made something good, we would certainly be proud of it. God looked at the world and said that it was good. Everything God did was good.

Sometimes we do things that are not so good. Because we do things that are not so good, we need forgiveness. Jesus died on the cross so that we could be forgiven for our sins. God gave up his only son for us. So we can see that God does love the whole entire world. What an awesome God we have!

Thank God for his love by bowing down to pray and worship Him.

John 3:16
For God so loved the world that he gave his only Son, so that everyone who believes in him may not perish but may have everlasting life.

Equipment

How many of you know your ABCs? How many know your multiplication tables? I want you to go into a empty room and write them down. When you are finished, bring the written answers back to me.

You could not do this unless I gave you pencils and paper. You must be equipped for the task.

After Jesus' resurrection, He appeared to His disciples where they were gathered. He knew some of them doubted who He was, so He showed them the scars left from the nails that held Him to the cross. He then told them to go out into the world and teach others about His love for them. He knew they could not do it alone, so He breathed The Holy Spirit upon them.

He gave us His love by dying on the cross for our sins. He gave us The Holy Spirit to equip us to teach others about Him. He does not send us out helpless. He is always there for us through The Holy Spirit.

The next time you prepare for a task, remember the Holy Spirit that Jesus has given to us for a helper.

John 20:21–22
Jesus said to them again, "Peace be with you. As the Father has sent me, so I send you." When he had said this, he breathed on them and said to them, "Receive the Holy Spirit."

Eye of the Mind

How many eyes do you have? You say you have two, but did you know that you have three eyes? Guess where the third eye is located. No, it isn't in your heart, but that was a close guess. The third eye is located in the mind.

This old washboard reminds me of my childhood. I can close my eyes and see my mother and me washing clothes at the spring. Thinking of my school reminds me of my younger days. The school has been torn down, but I can close my eyes and see it with my mind's eye. The look of the school has been recorded in my memory.

We can close our eyes and see things as they are in our memories. I'm sure the disciples of Jesus could close their eyes and see Jesus hanging on the cross for them.

The Bible was written and passed on through peoples' eyes of the mind. Jesus wanted us to record His words in our minds so that we could pass them on to future generations. The Bible tells us to have the mind of Christ in us and to pass it on.

Record the words of Christ in your mind; it will help you to see as Christ sees.

1 Corinthians 3:16
"For who has known the mind of the Lord so as to instruct him?" But we have the mind of Christ.

Faith and Trust

I want you to stand up in a line with your backs to me. As I ask each of you to fall back, I will catch you. Do you think I will let you fall onto the floor? Those of you who don't trust me may sit down.

Oh! I have four takers. What made you stay? You knew without a doubt that I would surely catch you. I'm glad you had faith in me. You depended on me to catch you without me proving it.

The Bible says that you can't please God without faith, that is, without depending upon Him. Anyone who wants to come to God must believe that there is a God and that He rewards those who truly look to Him.

Noah and Abraham trusted God to do what He said He would do. Sarah and many other people in the Bible trusted God.

Remember to put your faith and trust in God.

Hebrews 11:1
Now faith is the assurance of things hoped for, the conviction of things not seen.

Fiery Furnace

King Nebuchadnezzar lived in Babylon a very long time ago. He was very powerful and the people listened to him. He made a huge statue of gold, and told the people to bow down and worship it. If anyone refused to worship the statue, they would be thrown into a fiery furnace.

We don't worship statues, because we have learned we have a real living God to bow down to.

There were three men named Shadrah, Meshach, and Abednego, who would not bow down to the golden statue. The king became very angry because they would not bow down. He had them brought to him to give them another chance to bow down to the statue. Again, they would not bow down.

What would you have done?

The three men told the king that if they were put into the fiery furnace their God would protect them. They were mighty brave and courageous. The soldiers tied up Shadrach, Meshach, and Abednego, and threw them into the furnace.

Guess what happened? The three men didn't get burned or even scorched at all. It was amazing; the king could not believe his very own eyes. He saw four men in the furnace instead of three. God was protecting the three men.

The king ordered the men out of the furnace. He began to praise the God of Shadrach, Meshach, and Abednego. The king made a law that no one could say anything about their God. There was no other God who could save His people like this.

What a great and glorious God we have.

Always stand up for what is right; God will always be there to help you if you do.

Daniel 3:28

Nebuchadnezzar said, "Blessed be the God of Shadrach, Meshach, and Abednego, who has sent his angel and delivered his servants who trusted in him. They disobeyed the king's command and yielded up their bodies rather than serve and worship any god except their own God."

Fishers of Men

Don't step back now. I am going to see how many of you I can catch in this fishing net.

Just as I threw my net several of you stepped away and didn't get caught.

There are twenty of you and I only caught twelve. Some of you listened and stayed put, and some of you heard and stepped back. This is what happened when Jesus was calling His disciples. Some decided to come with Him. Jesus said He would make them "fishers of men."

Jesus needed people to help Him spread the Good News. Let's learn a song to the tune of "Bringing in the Sheaves."

There were twelve disciples Jesus called to help him,
Simon, Peter, Andrew, James his brother John.
Phillip, Thomas, Matthew, James the son of Alphaeus,
Thaddaeus, and Judas, and Bartholomew.
He has called us too,
He has called us too,
We are his disciples,
I am one and you.
He has called us too,
He has called us too,
We are his disciples,
I am one and you.

Follow Jesus and tell others about Him. This will make you one of His disciples.

Matthew 4:19–20
And he said to them, "Follow me, and I will make you fish for people." Immediately they left their nets and followed him.

Fishes and Loaves

Why are twelve baskets setting on the floor? After I tell you the story you can see that they represent a miracle.

Large crowds of people were following Jesus around, listening to His teachings. The disciples urged Jesus to send the people away because it was toward evening and there was no food. Instead of sending them away Jesus told the disciples to feed the crowd.

There was a boy there with five loaves of bread and two fish. He gave them to the disciples. There were about five thousand people to feed. Jesus told everyone to sit on the ground, and they did. He took the five loaves and two fish, looked up into the sky, and gave thanks. He then gave the bread and fish to the disciples to pass out.

Everyone ate and ate until they were full, but there were still twelve baskets of scraps left over. Can you imagine what surprise came over the peoples' faces? A miracle had taken place right before their very eyes. Jesus did many other miracles while He was here on earth.

Read the Bible and learn about the other miracles of Jesus.

Luke 9:13
But he said to them, "You give them something to eat." They said, "We have no more than five loaves and two fish—unless we are to go and buy food for these people."

Free Gift

Have you ever gotten a free gift? What does "free" mean? It means you didn't have to do any work for it, and you don't do anything at all for it.

Here is a free gift for each of you; all you have to do is accept it. You may open your gift box and see what is inside. It is a wooden cross made of olive wood from Jerusalem.

Someone usually gives you a gift because they love you. What is the biggest and best gift you have gotten? It shows you are special to someone.

The Bible tells us that God gave us His only Son as a gift. He loved us so much that He wanted us to have eternal life. We didn't have to pay Him anything to do this for us.

For us to have eternal life we have to accept God's free gift. We were bought with a price. Jesus died on the cross so that we could have eternal life.

Remember this the next time you see a cross.

Romans 6:23
For the wages of sin is death, but the free gift of God is eternal life in Christ Jesus our Lord.

Garden

What do you do when you are lonely? You long for someone to talk to or play with. After God created the heavens and the earth and all the animals, He was lonely. He wanted creatures that He could share His love with. He created a man and a woman, Adam and Eve, and placed them in a beautiful garden. He created them to live forever.

He told them they could eat anything in the garden except the fruit of one tree. God told Adam and Eve that if they ate the forbidden fruit, they would die.

Satan came to Eve in the form of a snake. The snake told Eve that she would not die if she ate the forbidden fruit. Eve believed the snake instead of God. Eve ate the fruit and offered some to Adam. Adam also decided to eat the forbidden fruit. Adam and Eve had disobeyed God. Sin had come into God's beautiful world.

Adam and Eve were made to leave the beautiful garden and make a living for themselves. They would no longer live forever.

However, God loved us so much that He prepared a way so we can still have eternal life. He sent His only Son, Jesus, to die for our sins. Life can spring forth out of death because of God's plan for us. Even a dead seed can spring forth and make a beautiful flower. Once we accept Jesus into our hearts, we have eternal life.

The next time somebody wants you to do something wrong, remember the story of Adam and Eve.

Genesis 2:8
And the Lord God planted a garden in Eden, in the East; and there he put man whom he had formed.

Gideon

Here is an empty jar and a torch. Objects such as these had a part in defeating the Midianites. The Midianites had control over the Israelites for seven years. The Israelites were tired of their control. Listen to the story.

One day, an Israelite by the name of Gideon was pounding grain in hiding because he didn't want the Midianites to see him. The Midianites were stealing from the Israelites and bullying them around. God spoke to Gideon and told him he was a mighty warrior and that He would help him to defeat the Midianites. Gideon didn't think he was a mighty warrior. God told him to take an army and go into battle with the Midianites.

Gideon took thirty-two thousand men, but God told him that was too many. God told Gideon to let the ones who were afraid go home. Twenty-two thousand men went home. God again told Gideon that his army was too large. God told Gideon to divide the men by letting them drink water. Three hundred men lapped water and the rest drank from their hands. Gideon sent the ones who drank from their hands home, leaving three hundred men. Gideon didn't think he could win the battle with three hundred men. God told Gideon and his men to take empty jars and torches and surround the enemy. At the same time, they were to burst the jars and shout at the top of their lungs.

The enemy was so scared they ran away. Surely Gideon had nothing to do with the defeat, but he had obeyed God. What an awesome God we have.

Remember that you can do anything through God who strengthens you.

Judges 6:16
The Lord said to him, "But I will be with you, and you shall strike down the Midianites, every one of them."

Giving

I have here a ten-cent piece, a one dollar bill, a ten dollar bill, and a one hundred dollar bill. I couldn't find a thousand dollar bill.

Once there was a man who made ten cents a week. He didn't mind giving one penny to the church. Then he made one dollar and didn't mind giving ten cents to the church. Next, he made ten dollars and didn't mind giving one dollar to the church. After that he made one hundred dollars and he reluctantly gave ten dollars to the church. Finally, he made one thousand dollars and gave only ten dollars, instead of one hundred dollars.

The more money the man made the greedier he got. Why did he do this? He had pledged to give ten percent of his earnings to the church. Wasn't this the same God who gave him the strength to earn all the money? It seems he didn't really want to take his promise seriously. Jesus said, "If you give little you will receive little." God loves a cheerful giver.

A farmer who plants just a few seeds will only get a small crop. Everyone must make up their mind as to how much they want to give. Cheerful givers are the ones God prizes. The Bible says, "The godly man gives generously to the poor." His good deeds will be an honor to Him forever.

Remember this the next time you earn some money.

2 Corinthians 9:6
The point is this: he who sows sparingly will also reap sparingly, and the one who sows bountifully will also reap bountifully.

God's Armor

Have you ever seen a vest as heavy as this one? Try it on and see how heavy it feels on your body. This is a policeman's bulletproof vest. It protects the upper part of his body, close to his heart. If a bullet hits the vest, the bullet doesn't hurt the officer.

Did you know God has provided us with an evil-proof vest? The vest God tells us to wear will keep sin out of our hearts. He gives us armor to protect us. The Bible says to put on the breastplate of God's approval, shoes that move you to teach about Him, the faith shield to stop Satan's fiery arrows, the helmet of salvation, and the sword of the Spirit. The sword of the Spirit symbolizes the Word of God.

He tells us to use every piece of His armor to resist the enemy when they attack.

When the battle is over, we will be the winner. Just as the vest protects the policeman, God has given us His armor to use. We should pray in times of trouble and ask God to help us.

Use your Bible to find out more about God's armor.

Ephesians 6:11
Put on the whole armor of God, so that you may be able to stand the wiles of the devil.

Gold

I have here two pieces of rock. Look at them very closely and tell me what you see. Yes, it looks like gold. Well, I thought it was gold also, so I took it to a jeweler to be tested. Guess what it turned out to be? It turned out to be fool's gold. It looks exactly like gold, but I wasn't satisfied until I heard it with my own two ears from the jeweler.

Do you know what gold is worth? About three hundred dollars an ounce, but it isn't worth more than anything in this world.

You probably have something more precious in your home. Do you know what it is? In Psalm 19 in your Bible it says that God's Word is more precious than gold and sweeter than honey.

See, we have a gold mine before our very own eyes. May God help us to read the Bible everyday and be thankful.

Go gold mining this week and read God's Word.

Psalms 19:10
More to be desired are they than gold, even much fine gold; sweeter also than honey, and drippings of the honeycomb.

Hearing

Now, what do you suppose this tiny device is? No, it is not a battery, but it has a very tiny battery on the inside of it. It is called a hearing aid. It helps some people hear better when they insert it into their ear.

Sometimes it is hard to hear sounds because they are not loud enough or we have something wrong with our inner ear. Do we hear all sounds? Do we hear when God calls us? What would help us to hear God's call?

Whether or not we hear God's call depends on the condition of our ears. Many are called by God, but only a few hear. Men of old heard God's voice and followed His advice. God called Abraham to go to a strange and foreign land. Abraham was obedient to God's call.

We can open our ears to God's call by being willing to seek Him through prayer and devotion. When we listen to God, He makes it possible for us to do the things He wants us to do. We should read and tell others about God, because faith comes from hearing and listening. The call of God is not for a few, but for everyone.

Keep your ears in tune so you can hear God calling you.

Genesis 12:1
Now the Lord said to Abram, "Go from your country and your kindred and your father's house to the land that I will show you."

High Tower

Here is a box of blocks. Let's see how high we can stack them. We can do better than that; let's try again. That's better, but they came tumbling down again. We don't get them stacked very high before they tumble down again.

Once man thought he could build a tower to reach the sky. At that time, people only spoke one language. They began to build the tower to reach the sky, but they were proud and wanted praise for themselves.

God did not want them to be too proud and boast of what they did, so He gave them different languages. They could no longer communicate, so the tower was not finished. The city was called Babel, meaning "confusion." The people of Babel were praising themselves instead of God, so God scattered them all over the world.

We are to have faith in God and let Him be our strong tower. He said He was the cornerstone of all people. The lesson to be learned here is to never put ourselves before God.

Remember this the next time you try to build a tower out of blocks.

Genesis 11:4
Then they said, "Come, let us build ourselves a city, and a tower with its top in the heavens, and let us make a name for ourselves; lest we be scattered abroad upon the face of the whole earth."

Holy Spirit

I'm going to turn this fan on high speed. My, that's a lot of air blowing in here. What would you think if you felt this much air blowing on you and there was no fan around? Would you wonder where the wind came from?

Seven weeks after the resurrection of Jesus, His believers met together. During their meeting, suddenly there was a sound like the roaring of a mighty windstorm in the skies above them, and it filled the room where they were meeting. Everyone present was filled with the Holy Spirit.

Jesus had promised the disciples that this would happen. They did not know, however, that the Spirit would come in the form of a windstorm. The Holy Spirit made them bold and courageous. The disciples began preaching and teaching as Jesus had told them to do. The Holy Spirit helped the Gospel spread throughout the world.

This day is called Pentecost, the birthday of the church. The Holy Spirit lives in us to help us overcome evil.

Remember this the next time you feel the cool breeze of a fan. Think of God as being inside of you.

Acts 2:2
And suddenly a sound came from heaven like the rush of a mighty wind, and it filled all the entire house where they were sitting.

How Much is Enough?

Look at this chart. Do you know what a chart shows? The dictionary says a chart is a "sheet giving any kind of information in lists, pictures, tables or diagrams." The highest point on this chart is 100%. We can measure many things by using a chart. A chart can compare what we did yesterday to what we do today.

Let's use this chart to show how much we love Jesus. If we read the Bible, pray, or attend church about half of the time, we would color the chart on the 50% mark. If we don't read the Bible, pray, or attend church, we would color the chart on the 0% mark. Let's see where we all fit on the chart for loving Jesus.

The Bible tells us we must love Jesus 100%. We must love Him more than our own family. We cannot be one of Jesus' disciples if we do not go 100%. To love Him 100% we must give Him our heart and give up all our selfish desires. We must love others more than ourselves. We must let Jesus be in control of our lives.

Even though we may not yet be at the 100% mark, we can work toward this goal. Jesus gave 100% when He died on the cross for our sins. Jesus is not satisfied unless we give 100% of ourselves.

Remember how much God loves you the next time you see a chart.

Luke 14:26
"Whoever comes to me and does not hate father and mother, wife and children, brothers and sisters, yes, and even life itself, cannot be my disciple."

Living Water

See this glass of water; look how dirty and muddy the water looks. The water is not fit to be used. Look at what happens when I continually pour clear, clean water into the dirty water. The more clear water I pour into the glass, the clearer the water gets. Finally all the dirty water has overflowed out and the glass is full of clear water, ready to be used.

Jesus was on his way to Galilee and went through Samaria. He stopped at Jacob's well to rest while his disciples went into town for food. While He was at the well, a Samaritan woman came to draw water from the well. Jesus asked her for a drink of water. She asked why a Jew would ask her for a drink of water. Jews and Samaritans did not share with one another. Jesus told the Samaritan woman that if she had asked Him for water, He could have given her living water and she would never thirst again. She would be continually supplied with living water.

The Word of God is like fresh water that cleanses our soul of sin and fills us with a new way of life. The truth and the Word of God changes us. The more we learn about Jesus, the more we can become like Him. The truth can cleanse us and set us free from sin.

Every time you drink fresh cool water, think of Jesus as being living water.

John 4:10
Jesus answered her, "If you knew the gift of God, and who it is that is saying to you, 'Give me a drink,' you would have asked him, and he would have given you living water."

Look Inside!

Look at this pineapple; see how rough and uneven it is. If you aren't careful how you touch it or pick it up, you will get stuck. Look at this kiwi fruit, it is all fuzzy and brown-looking.

Would you take a bite of either of these fruits, as they are, with the peel still on? No, by no means. Now here are the fruits peeled and prepared to eat. Take a piece of each and see how good each piece tastes. You can't always judge that something won't be good by looking at the outside of it.

Jesus taught us this by saying that He looks at what is inside of our hearts and minds. He does not judge us by the kind of clothes we wear or our appearance. We can have on shabby clothes and still show kindness and love to one another. Jesus knows what kind of people we are.

Remember this the next time you eat a piece of fruit.

Matthew 7:1
"Do not judge, so that you may not be judged."

Lost and Found

Sixty years ago the ruby set in this ring was lost by my mother. The ruby was precious to her because my father had given it to her when she was sixteen years old. It was lost for about two years.

One day I was playing on the floor in the kitchen. I saw something deep pink under the stove. I thought it was a fire coal so I took a straw from the broom and dragged it out.

I ran to my mother with the ruby and she was overjoyed. Have you ever lost something that was precious to you? How did you feel when you found it?

Jesus told us of the excitement and joy felt when a woman found one of her lost coins. Jesus is always searching for one who is lost in sin. He is our Shepherd; He watches over us. Jesus said that there is joy in heaven when one sinner repents.

The next time you lose something, think about how Jesus searches for you if you are lost.

Luke 15:10
"Just so, I tell you, there is joy in the presence of the angels of God over one sinner who repents."

Love of Money

I have here some bills of paper money. What does money buy? Food, clothes, shelter, entertainment? Yes, these are some of the things money can buy.

Some people love to have money just to say they have it. They sometimes get the money in a dishonest way. Some people who long to be rich do all kinds of things to get money.

The Bible tells us we should not love money. The Bible tells us that money, or the love of money, does not make us truly happy. What makes us truly rich? The Bible tells us to work for what is right and good, to trust God, to love others, and to be patient and gentle. We should use our money to do good. We should do good works and give happily to those in need, and always be ready to share with others.

By doing these things we will be storing up treasures in heaven. What money can't buy Jesus gives us freely. He did this when He died on the cross for our sins. He gave us eternal life, which no amount of money can buy.

Remember this the next time you handle money.

1 Timothy 6:10
For the love of money is a root of all kinds of evil, and in their eagerness to be rich some have wandered away from the faith and pierced themselves with many pains.

Map

Where would you like to go today on a long trip? Name a place and we will look at this map of the United States to see how we can get there. You picked Disney World in Orlando, Florida. Let's find where we are on the map. Here it is—Efland, North Carolina.

By looking at the map we could get on Interstate 40 East and go to Interstate 95. Then we would take exit 86, drive on Interstate 4 to Orlando, and follow Disney signs. This map makes it easier for us.

How do we get to heaven? Could we find our way by looking at this map? The Bible says Jesus is "the way, the truth, and the life." Jesus said He would prepare a way for us. He prepared a way by dying on the cross for our sins so that we could go to heaven. We find the way by reading the Bible as our map, praying, and following Jesus' Will for our lives.

The next time you see a map, think about following Jesus' route.

John 14:6
Jesus said to him, "I am the way, and the truth, and the life. No one comes to the Father, except through me."

Millstones

Lift this stone and see how heavy it is. It is small, but it weighs about one pound. Here is a picture of a millstone that was dug up from some ruins in the town of Caesarea, a town on the coast of the Mediterranean Sea in Israel.

Millstones were much heavier than the stone I have here. They had to be heavy, because in the past they were used to grind grain. Millstones were so heavy that farmers had to use donkeys to pull them.

Jesus was teaching His disciples one day on the hillside. There were children playing nearby. Some of the disciples wanted the children to go away, but Jesus said, "Let the little children come to Me." Jesus loves everyone, young or old.

Another time Jesus warned the people against tempting children into sin. He said the one tempting would be better off if he were thrown into the sea "with a millstone around his neck."

So you see how Jesus feels about little children. You are very special to Him. He loves you all.

Remember this the next time you pick up a heavy stone.

Luke 17:2
"It would be better for you if a millstone were hung round your neck and you were thrown into the sea than for you to cause one of these little ones to stumble."

Mustard Seed

I have here a handful of seeds, some large, some small, and some very tiny. Which one of these seeds do you think will make the biggest plant? The grain of corn will make a tall stalk. The watermelon seed will make a plant that runs on the ground. This acorn will make a large tree. The smallest seed I have here is a mustard seed. It is so tiny you can hardly see it, but it makes a very large plant.

A seed doesn't have to be large to make a large plant. Small things are sometimes more important than large things. You may have heard it said that it is the small things we do that make a difference.

The disciples were trying to cast out a demon from a young boy and could not do it. Jesus told them it was because they lacked faith. He told them if they had faith, even an amount as small as a tiny mustard seed, nothing would be impossible for them to do.

We increase our faith by learning about Jesus and what He did. How can we be like Jesus if we don't learn about Him?

Read the Bible and pray every day. The next time you see a seed, think about faith and what it can help you do.

Matthew 17:20
He said to them, "Because of your little faith. For truly, I tell you, if you have faith the size of a mustard seed, you will say to this mountain, 'Move from here to there,' and it will move; and nothing will be impossible for you."

Neighbors

Here is a Band-Aid. Have you ever had to use one? I'm sure you have. They are for minor cuts and bruises. Children tend to think they feel much better after a Band-Aid is applied. It shows someone cares when they have their wound all cleaned up and a Band-Aid applied. A person would certainly do this little thing for someone if they were loving and kind.

Jesus told a parable about a man lying in a ditch who had been beaten up by a robber and left to die. No small Band-Aid could fix him up. He must have been in pretty bad shape, because the robbers left him there to die. Two people passed him by and did not offer to help him. Then along came a Samaritan man who had compassion for him. The Samaritan bound up the man's wounds, put him on his beast, and took him to the nearest inn.

The next day when he left, the Samaritan gave the innkeeper enough money to finish taking care of the injured man. This was really being a good neighbor.

Jesus would want us to do the very same thing for one who is hurt. He said for us to go and do likewise.

Think about the Good Samaritan the next time you apply a Band-Aid.

Luke 10:36–37

"Which of these three, do you think, was a neighbor to the man who fell into the hands of the robbers?" He said, "The one who showed him may." Jesus said to him, "Go and do likewise."

New Ground

Breaking new ground is harder than plowing ground that has been plowed before. The plow is easier to use than this mattock or this shovel. Stumps, roots, rocks, and clods are hard to remove, but it is necessary to remove them in order to have a good harvest.

Jesus sent out seventy men ahead of him in pairs to every town and place where He intended to go. He told them, "The harvest is plentiful, but the laborers are few." He wanted them to be laborers to help the people know who Jesus was.

Old ideas and prejudices had to be removed to make way for Jesus. Just like getting stumps and rocks out of the ground, the men were going to have a hard time getting the people to listen.

People in many towns refused to listen. Jesus told them that if the people did not listen in one town, they should go on to another town. They were to try to get in a good harvest.

When you talk to someone about Jesus and they won't listen, don't let it discourage you from telling someone else.

Luke 10:16
"Whoever listens to you listens to me, and whoever rejects you rejects me, and whoever rejects me rejects the one who sent me."

Nicodemus

One night a man approached Jesus. He had his head partially covered and he was carrying a light. Jesus could barely see who he was. Jesus finally realized it was Nicodemus, who was a Jew and a Pharisee. He was a keeper of the law, and a moral and upright man. The Pharisees recognized Jesus as a teacher but did not worship or recognize Him as being God. They knew nothing of God's love. Nicodemus was seeking answers to questions. The Pharisees did not go along with the teachings of Jesus. Their religious beliefs were different. He did not want the other Pharisees to see him.

Nicodemus asked Jesus what he must do to have eternal life. Jesus told him he must be "born from above." Jesus told Nicodemus that outwardly keeping the law wasn't enough. To be born again means letting the Spirit of God live in you. The truth is made visible by a change of everyday life that comes from the presence of the Spirit of God. The way we live shows if God is present in our lives.

Remember to show God's love by the way you act and what you say.

John 3:3
Jesus answered him "Very truly, I tell you, no one can see the kingdom of God without being born from above."

Old Shirt

What is the difference in these two shirts? You are right; one is old-looking and one is new. The new one still has the tags on it.

Sometimes we clean out our closets to get rid of some of the old stuff. We usually give the clothes to someone who needs them, or to a charitable organization. They are too good to throw away. If we were giving one of these shirts to Jesus, which one would we want to give? The new one, of course, because Jesus deserves the best from us. If we would give Jesus the new one, why not give a needy person the new one? Jesus said that doing something for someone else is the same as doing something for Him.

The righteous asked Jesus if they had ever seen Him hungry, thirsty, naked, or in need. Jesus told them that seeing people in need of any of these things is the same as seeing Him in need.

Remember to treat everyone as you would treat Jesus.

Matthew 25:35–36, Matthew 25:40
"For I was hungry and you gave me food, I was thirsty and you gave me something to drink, I was a stranger and you welcomed me, I was naked and you gave me clothing, I was sick and you took care of me, I was in prison and you visited me."

"Truly, I say to you, as you did it to one of the least of these who are members of my family, you did it to me."

One God

What did Jesus mean when He said that He and His Father were one? How can He be more than one person? That is something that can be hard for us to understand, but we believe it because of our faith in the Word.

The Bible says the Word existed in the very beginning. It also says that the Word was God, and the Word became like a man and lived among people. Trinity means "three in one." God is The Father, The Son, and The Holy Spirit.

Let's look to see if we can make it easier to understand. Water consists of two parts hydrogen and one part oxygen. Ice consists of two parts hydrogen and one part oxygen. Steam consists of two parts hydrogen and one part oxygen. So you see, two parts hydrogen and one part oxygen can be in three forms, and yet be the same. So why should we doubt that God, as all-powerful as He is, could not be the same? He made ice, water, and steam.

He said for us not to trust our own understanding, but instead to trust what God says. God revealed Himself through Jesus and when Jesus left the Earth He left The Holy Spirit to dwell within us.

Remember, you always have a part of God within you. Remember this the next time you see water, ice, or steam.

1 John 10:30
"I and the Father are one."

Oreos and Onions

Here is a platter containing things to eat. The platter contains Oreo cookies, celery, carrots and onions. Pass the platter around and you may take one of your choice.

Lauren took an Oreo cookie, Dana took an Oreo cookie, Kelsey took an Oreo cookie, Brandon took an Oreo cookie and Mary Beth took an Oreo cookie. Look at all the vegetables that are left! None of us picked a vegetable that we do not like. Sometimes things we don't like are good for us.

Sometimes we go through hard times and we learn lessons. When Jesus was in the garden praying, He asked God to take the cup of suffering from Him. However, He said He was willing to suffer if it was God's will. He suffered for us although it was hard for Him to do. He died on the cross for us.

Jesus was given a portion hard to swallow, but He went to the cross for us. Sometimes we have to swallow things that don't taste good but they can be good for us.

Remember this the next time you are asked to eat vegetables. Think how good they can be for you even if they are hard to swallow.

Matthew 26:39
And going a little farther, he threw himself on the ground and prayed, "My Father, if it is possible, let this cup pass from me; yet not what I want but what you want."

Perfume

What do we do if we are going to have special guest for a few days? We clean house, get groceries, and get out our best china and tablecloth. We want them to feel special. We also prepare for special holidays.

Many times the Bible tells us about Mary and Martha. Martha was always busy cleaning and preparing meals for Jesus. Mary always took up special time with Jesus. Once a banquet was prepared in Jesus' honor. Martha served as they sat at the table. Then Mary took a jar of expensive perfume and poured it on Jesus' feet. She then wiped His feet with her hair. The house was filled with the fragrance. Then Judas, the disciple who was to betray Jesus, said, "That perfume was worth a fortune; it should have been sold and the money given to the poor."

Jesus replied, "Let her alone, she did it for My going away. You can always help the poor, but I won't be with you always."

Mary was letting Jesus know He was special and was worth more than the perfume. She gave her most expensive gift to Jesus.

Do we give Him our best or just very little? Think about this; what do you think Jesus is worth? A small dab of perfume or a whole bottle?

Always remember to give Jesus your best.

John 12:3
Mary took a pound of costly perfume made of pure nard, anointed Jesus' feet and wiped them with her hair. The house was filled with the fragrance of the perfume.

Persistence

One day Jesus told a parable to teach us to pray and never give up praying. There was once a widow woman who went before a judge to get justice against her opponent. The judge was not a caring person. When the widow asked for justice, the judge turned her away—not once but several times. Still the widow came back asking the judge to help her. The judge finally gave in and gave her justice, but only because he didn't want to be bothered with her anymore. The widow was persistent in asking the judge for help.

The Bible tells us that if a non-caring person gave in to her wishes, a caring person would help her much more easily. God wants us to come to Him in prayer persistently. He wants companionship with us through prayer.

Remember to pray, and never give up praying.

Luke 18:1
Then Jesus told them a parable about their need to pray always and not to lose heart.

Peter's Denial

Isn't this a pretty rooster? It is made of colored popcorn and pinto beans. My daughter made this when she was in Bible school.

Real roosters crow early in the morning at the crack of dawn. They remind me of a Bible story.

Peter was one of Jesus' closest disciples. One day Peter told Jesus that he would always stick by Him, even until death. Jesus told Peter that he would deny Him not once, but three times before the cock crowed.

When Jesus was on trial Peter lingered back in the crowd because he thought he might get arrested also. He was standing in the courtyard warming by a fire when someone recognized him as one of Jesus' disciples. Peter denied knowing who Jesus was three times. Immediately, the cock crowed and Peter remembered Jesus' words. He became very sorry for what he had done.

Sometimes we pretend we don't know who Jesus is by not standing up for Him. We deny Jesus when we have an opportunity to do good and we don't do it. We deny Jesus when we don't offer a smile to someone who is sad. We all have been like Peter, but Jesus is always forgiving and kind.

Remember to be more like Jesus and not deny Him.

Luke 22:34

Jesus said, "I tell you, Peter, the cock will not crow this day, until you have denied three times that you know me."

Plow

Do you know what this is? No, it's not part of a shovel, but it is a small plow share. It is used to turn the soil over. When I was a young girl we lived on a farm and had no tractor. My dad would use a plow pulled by a mule to plow the fields.

I loved to see and smell the fresh new earth turned over and look down the straight rows. I often wondered how the rows were so straight. He would focus on the end of the row and look straight ahead, never looking back. Do you know what would have happened if he had looked back? He would have lost his focus and the row would not have been straight.

As I got older, the words of Jesus would come to mind when I thought of my father's plowing. Jesus once told a young man that if he was committed to following Him, he must never look back.

Once we are committed to Christ we must not turn back to our former way of doing things. If we try to live our lives in the past, we can't enjoy the future. The only way a task can be finished is to look forward.

Keep your eyes, mind, and heart on Jesus. Read the Bible and pray, and God will direct your path.

Luke 9:62

Jesus said to him, "No one who puts a hand to the plow and looks back is fit for the kingdom of God."

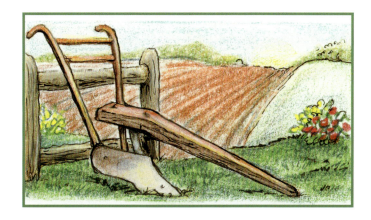

Potter's Clay

Here is a piece of clay for each of you. Try to make a very small jug. If you don't get it right the first time, mash the clay back together and start all over again. This is what a potter does with clay that he works with. Sometimes he does it many times before he gets it to look the way he wants it to look.

Jesus said that in His hands we are like the clay in a potter's hands. Jesus said "I can do to you what the potter has done to his clay."

Jesus can mold us and make us perfect. If we make a mistake, He will forgive us and we can start all over again. When broken, He can mend us back together just as we can glue a broken piece of pottery. He is eager to forgive and forget our mistakes. He died on the cross for our sins.

The next time you break something, remember you are clay in Jesus' hands.

Jeremiah 18:5–6

Then the word of the Lord came to me: "Can I not do with you, O house of Israel, as this potter has done? says the Lord; Behold, like the clay in the potter's hand, so are you in my hand, O house of Israel."

Prayer

How do we know Jesus learned to pray when He was growing up? When He was an adult He prayed, which shows that He learned to pray when He was a child.

Jesus prayed in the Garden of Gethsemane. He prayed all night long until drops of blood fell from His forehead. His disciples fell asleep while He was praying. He prayed for Jerusalem. He prayed for the thieves who hung on crosses beside Him. He even prayed that God would forgive the ones responsible for His hanging on the cross to die for our sins.

Surely we can learn to pray if we are going to be like Jesus. It should be a part of our everyday lives. Jesus taught His disciples the Lord's Prayer as a model for us to go by.

Learn the Lord's Prayer and use it as a model when you pray. Praying will help you be obedient to His will.

Matthew 6:9–13

"Pray then in this way: Our Father in heaven, hallowed be your name. Your kingdom come, Your will be done, on earth as it is in heaven. Give us this day our daily bread. And forgive us our debts, as we have also forgiven our debtors. And do not bring us to the time of trial, but rescue us from the evil one."

Prodigal Son

This suitcase contains things I would take if I went on a trip for a while. Let's name some of them. Toothbrush, toothpaste, comb, shirts, pants, shoes, socks, underwear, camera, film, and maybe some snack foods.

We left out one thing we would need. That thing would be money.

Jesus told a story about a young man who took all of his belongings and the inheritance money he was to get and left home. After a short time he ran out of money, and he had nothing to eat. He found a job feeding pigs. He was even eating the pigs' food. He remembered how much he had to eat when he was at home. He wondered if his father would take him back and let him be a hired servant.

He decided to go back home to his father's house and ask forgiveness for being so foolish. When he was still a long distance off his father saw him, was filled with joy, and ran to meet him. He asked his father to forgive him while they were embracing. His father did forgive him, and gave him a big party because the son was once lost but had been found.

Jesus is always ready to forgive us when we do something wrong if we ask Him. What a loving and wonderful God we have.

Remember to ask Jesus to forgive you when you do wrong.

Luke 15:20
So he set off and went to his father. But while he was still far off, his father saw him and was filled with compassion; he ran and put his arms around him and kissed him.

Race

I need four volunteers to enter a sack race. The rest of you will be cheerleaders. The first one to get to the big maple tree is the winner. The prize is behind the tree. If you fall down, get up and keep going until you get there.

Get set! Go! Well, we have a winner, but all of you tried very hard. What were you thinking during the race? You probably kept your mind and your eyes on the maple tree so that you could go straight to it and not get off course.

Let's try to think of life as one big race. The Bible tells us to keep focused on Jesus in our race of life. Only through Him will we receive the prize of eternal life. The prize is not only for the first one there, it is for all who put their trust in Him. We must keep focused on Him throughout our entire life.

To enter the race you must accept Jesus into your heart. So jump in your sack and go to it!

Hebrews 12:1–2
Therefore, since we are surrounded by so a great cloud of witnesses, let us also lay aside every weight, and the sin which clings so closely, and let us run with perseverance the race that is set before us, looking to Jesus the pioneer and perfecter of our faith, who for the sake of joy that was set before Him endured the cross, disregarding its shame, and has taken his seat at the right hand of the throne of God.

Rainbow

Look at all the beautiful colors in this picture of a rainbow. Do you know why God put a rainbow in the sky? Listen to the story.

A very long time ago evil had become so bad that God was very disappointed in almost all of the people on Earth. There was a man named Noah, however, that God was pleased with, because Noah loved God. God told Noah to build a big boat because there was going to be a great flood that would destroy all of mankind. He would need the boat, called an ark, to save his family and the animals of the world.

When the ark was ready God told Noah to enter with his wife, sons, and sons' wives, as well as two of every kind of animal.

It rained for forty days and forty nights. The ark was safe in the water. Those left on earth were destroyed by the great flood.

After a very long time in the ark, Noah sent out a dove to see if the water had gone down. When the dove returned with an olive leaf, Noah knew the land was beginning to dry out. God told Noah to leave the ark, take all the animals, and replenish the earth.

Noah built an altar to God and God was very pleased. God promised to never flood the whole Earth again. He set a rainbow in the sky as a reminder of His promise.

Whenever you see a rainbow, think of God's love.

Genesis 9:13

I have set my bow in the clouds, and it shall be a sign of the covenant between me and the earth.

Rubies

Do you know what I will be talking about today? You don't? Okay, today is Mother's Day, so let's talk about mothers. Do you think mothers are precious? You do and so do I.

I have a riddle for you to solve. I am wearing something that belonged to my mother and it is eighty years old. Can you guess what it is? "Bracelet" is a good guess, but that's not it. No, it's not my necklace either. Lauren guessed that it is the dress that I have on. It may look that old, but that's not correct either. I will give you a hint: the Bible says that mothers are more precious than this thing I am wearing. Okay, since you can't guess, I will tell you. It is a ruby ring that my father gave to my mother when she was sixteen.

The ring is precious to me but my mother was more precious. The Bible says mothers are more precious than rubies.

Honor your mothers today by doing something special for her.

Proverbs 3:15
She is more precious than jewels, and nothing you desire can compare with her.

Smell the Bread

Smell the warm loaf of bread. Pass it around, touch it, and smell it. Doesn't it make you hungry? Do you love to smell bread baking? This is one of the main foods we use in our diets. It has calcium, iron, vitamin A, niacin, thiamin, riboflavin, and folic acid. These things are all needed to sustain life and make us healthy.

No wonder Jesus said, at the Last Supper with His disciples, that He was the Bread of Life. It is He who sustains us through The Holy Spirit. He gave His body for us. We pass the loaf at Holy Communion because He said to do this in remembrance of Him.

He loved us so much He hung on the cross and died so that we could be forgiven for our sins.

Remember how much Jesus loves you when you smell the aroma of bread cooking and when you are eating bread.

Matthew 26:26
While they were eating, Jesus took a loaf of bread, and after blessing it he broke it, gave it to the disciples, and said, "Take, eat; this is my body."

Sower

A large crowd had gathered at the shore where Jesus was teaching. The crowd was so large that Jesus got into a boat and taught from it while the people listened on the beach.

He told the story of a farmer who was sowing grain in his fields. As the farmer sowed the seed, some fell beside the path and birds came and ate the seeds.

Some seeds fell on rocky soil where there was little dirt. Some of them came up as plants, but the sun scorched them and they withered and died because they had little root.

Other seeds fell among thorns, and the thorns choked them out.

Finally, some of the seeds fell on good soil, and produced an abundant crop.

Jesus told the crowd to listen to His explanation carefully. The hard path where some of the seeds fell represented the heart of a person who hears God's Word, but has it snatched away by Satan.

The rocky soil represented the heart of a person who hears God's message and receives it with joy, but doesn't have much depth because his faith is weak.

The ground covered with thorns represented a heart who hears but cares more about money and material things. The desire for these things chokes out God's Word.

The good ground represented the heart of someone who listens to the message and understands it. This type of person will bring many into the kingdom of God.

We can be the different types of soil the seeds fall upon. The best type to be like is the good soil.

Let Jesus' love be planted into your heart and let it multiply and be told to others.

Matthew 13:1–3
That same day Jesus went out of the house and sat beside the sea. Such great crowds gathered around Him that He got into a boat and sat there, while crowds gathered on the beach, And He told them many things in parables, saying: "Listen! a sower went out to sow."

Special Apples

One day my father was reading the newspaper and I came into the room. He looked up from his paper and said, "Joyce, you are my special child and I am going to give you a big red apple." When I was a child getting a big red apple was a special treat.

He told me not to tell my other sisters. I ran around the house to hide and eat my apple. As I ran around the corner of the house, I bumped into one of my sisters. She also had a big red apple. She didn't see my apple and she told me that my father had said she was special. I then showed her my apple and we ate together as special children.

Have you ever given something to someone because they were special? The Bible tells us that all people are God's special children. He made each one of us different and unique. He knew us even before we were born. We are the apple of His eye.

The next time someone does something special for you, think and know that you are God's special child.

1 John 3:1
See what love the Father has given us, that we should be called the children of God; and that is what we are.

Sponges

Here is a sponge. Do you know how sponges are used? But this one is hard and shriveled up. How can we clean up something with a hard, shriveled sponge? Oh! It needs to be soaked in water, you are right.

The water makes it soft so that it can do the job. If we wipe a surface with the hard sponge, the dirt is smeared and the surface doesn't get it clean. When we wipe a surface with a wet sponge, it removes the dirt very quickly. The water makes it useful. If we don't use it while it is wet, it dries back up and is not useful.

We can compare ourselves with a sponge. We soak up God's blessings everyday. If we fail to use them for something good or pass them along, we might as well not have had them in the first place. God gives us many fruits of the Spirit. The Bible says we are to use our gifts to help others.

Thank Him for His many blessings the next time you see a sponge being used.

John 15:8
My father is glorified by this, that you bear much fruit and become my disciples.

Stones

Look at the basket full of stones. What is different about these rocks? Yes, they do have words printed on them. Do rocks talk? Let's read some of the words printed on them: Praise the Lord, King of Kings, Hosanna, Blessed One, and Promised Messiah.

As Jesus was riding on a donkey into Jerusalem people began to rejoice and praise Him. Some of the Pharisees in the crowd asked Jesus to rebuke them; in other words, to tell the people to be quiet. Jesus said that if people wouldn't proclaim who He really was then the stones would cry out and let them know. Jesus wanted everyone to know who He was and why He came. He came to forgive our sins so that we could have eternal life.

Don't forget to praise Jesus for His blessings.

Luke 19:40
He answered, "I tell you, if these were silent, the stones would shout out."

Ten Commandments

Long ago God called a man by the name of Moses to lead his people out of slavery from Egypt. God spoke to Moses from a burning bush. The flame did not hurt the bush. He told Moses to go to Egypt and talk to the pharaoh, the leader of Egypt, about letting his people go. At first, the pharaoh would not agree to Moses' request. After ten plagues, or curses, happened to the people of Egypt, the pharaoh finally agreed to let the Hebrew slaves go free.

Moses had prayed for God to be with him. God had promised to be with Moses.

When the Hebrew people were leaving Egypt, God divided the waters of the Red Sea so they could get across. When the Egyptians came after them, they were drowned because God closed the water upon them.

Soon the Hebrew people came to a place called Mount Sinai. God spoke to Moses again and told him that the Hebrews would be a special people if they obeyed Him. God told Moses to go up to the mountain. He gave Moses rules for the Hebrew people to live by. God said it would please Him if they obeyed the rules. The rules would help the Hebrews live in a society where God would take care of them.

The rules were called the Ten Commandments. They were carved into two tablets of stone. God gave the tablets of stone to Moses when He called him up to the mountain.

Ten Commandments
(continued)

Always follow the Ten Commandments. They are God's Law.

1. Thou shalt have no other gods before me.
2. Thou shalt not make unto thee any graven image.
3. Thou shalt not take the name of the Lord in vain.
4. Remember the Sabbath Day, to keep it holy.
5. Honor thy father and thy mother.
6. Thou shalt not kill.
7. Thou shalt not commit adultery.
8. Thou shalt not steal.
9. Thou shalt not bear false witness against thy neighbor.
10. Thou shalt not covet.

Deuteronomy 5:22

These words the Lord spoke with a loud voice to your whole assembly at the mountain, out of fire, the cloud, and the thick darkness, and he added no more. He wrote them on two stone tablets, and gave them to me.

Thorns

Do you know what these are? Yes, they are very big thorns that came from a large thorn bush growing in Israel. I picked them from a bush when I was there. They grew wild all around the countryside where Jesus lived. Feel how hard and sticky they are. A very light touch to one of them would bring blood to your finger in an instant. These are probably the kinds of thorns used to make the crown for Jesus when He was put on the cross to die for us.

The Bible says the Roman soldiers placed the crown of thorns on Jesus' head and made fun of Him. They also made a sign that said *King of the Jews* and placed it above His head on the cross.

The next time you touch a thorn, remember how Jesus must have suffered for us with those large thorns sticking into His scalp. Remember to thank Him for dying so that we might have eternal life.

Matthew 27:29
And after twisting some thorns into a crown, they put it on his head. They put a reed in his right hand and knelt before him and mocked him, saying, "Hail, King of the Jews!"

Time

It's time to talk about time. This clock shows us a twelve-hour period. It can be A.M. for "after midnight" or P.M. for "before midnight." Who made time? God made time. He made night and day and all the seasons.

The Bible says that there is a time for all things. Sometimes we feel that there is not enough time in a day to do the things we want to do. God was all-wise when He made time; a time to be awake and a time to sleep. The Bible says a lot about time. There is a time to seek the Lord and a time to praise the Lord. We must use our time wisely and not waste it. Time is precious. The Bible also says that time is short. It says that God will help us in times of trouble and need. It says that there will come a time when time will be no more.

Do you know when this time will be? It will be when we get to heaven, because in heaven there is no need for time, for there is no day or night. It is time to remember who our maker is and praise Him.

The next time you look at a clock, remember that God made the beginning of time.

Ecclesiastes 3:1
For everything there is a season, and a time for every matter under heaven.

Title

Let's look at this piece of paper and see if you can tell me what it is. At the top of the page it is written: TITLE OF CERTIFICATE. It shows that I am the owner of a car and gives the description of the car.

If we own something of value we usually have a title of certificate for it. Did you know you are owned by someone with your name on a title of certificate? Guess who owns you?

The great apostle Paul wrote to the Corinthians and told the people that God owned them. How? He put His brand upon them—His mark of ownership—and gave them His Holy Spirit in their hearts as a guarantee that they belonged to Him. This was the first installment of all that He was going to give them. Indeed, He has given this gift to all of us.

It is God who made us, so why shouldn't we belong to Him? He wants to use us to tell others about His love. He wants us to proclaim His good news to everyone.

The next time you see a title of certificate remember who you belong to.

2 Corinthians 1:21-22
But it is God who establishes us with you in Christ and has anointed us, by putting his seal on us and giving us his Spirit in our hearts as a first installment.

Transformation

This cocoon was found hanging on a tree in my backyard. Inside is the larvae of an insect in the pupa stage. The larvae transforms into a caterpillar and then changes into a beautiful butterfly like the one in this picture.

This change is called "metamorphosis"; my, what a big word for you. Big changes take place in the development of a butterfly. The pupa is completely transformed.

We can compare our lives with this transformation. When we live in sin, we are not living in a relationship with Jesus. Jesus can take away our sin and make us a new person. We can become something wonderful and beautiful like a butterfly when we let Jesus into our hearts. No wonder a butterfly is a symbol for new birth.

The next time you see a butterfly, think about the changes that took place in them and what Jesus can do for you.

2 Corinthians 5:17
So if anyone is in Christ, there is a new creation: everything old has passed away; see, everything has become new!

Treasure Box

Let's see what is in this treasure box. I see a pearl necklace, a ruby ring, a gold coin, a silver chain, a gold watch that belonged to my father, and a cameo pin. These are things I want to keep because they mean something to me.

Someone could break into my house and steal this box. Jesus said that we should store up treasures that no man can steal. He said to first seek the kingdom of God and all else would be given to us. He said where our treasures are, our hearts are there also.

If we put our faith in Him, He gives us all we need. He feeds the birds of the air, and He cares much more for us.

Learn all you can about what Jesus teaches and treasure this in your heart.

Luke 12:34
"For where your treasure is, there will be your heart also."

True Vine

Here is a blackberry vine full of blackberries. The fruit looks very delicious. If it were not for the vine and branches, there would be no fruit. The berries are on the long branches. The branches get their food from the main part of the vine. When the branches die they have to be cut back in order to preserve the rest of the plant.

Jesus told His disciples that He was the true vine. He said every branch must bear fruit or it will be taken away, and every branch that bears fruit is pruned so that it can bear more fruit. He said He was the vine and we are the branches. The good fruits we must bear for Him are: love, joy, peace, patience, kindness, goodness, faithfulness, gentleness, and self control. If we depend on Jesus, we can produce these good fruits. Every one of us can be branches for Jesus.

The next time you eat fruit, remember Jesus is the true vine and we are the branches that produce good fruit.

John 15:1
"I am the true vine, and my father is the vinedresser."

Two Flower Baskets

See this hanging basket! I found it while looking for a basket in which to plant a flower. I keep soil and baskets on a table behind an old building. The plant has only a few stems left. But look! I see a little green leaf trying to burst open. What do you think it would take for this flower to bloom again? Water . . . sun . . . plant food. You are absolutely right, because look!

I have another basket here that was in the very same shape. Look how beautiful it is now. I gave it exactly what you said it needed: water, plant food, and sunlight. Sometimes we get like the dead-looking plant. We are lazy, not wanting to read the Bible or pray.

The Bible is food for our soul and keeps us in touch with God. We need to be beautiful for Him and let our light shine into other peoples' lives. Jesus can do just that for us if we stay in His Word. Jesus is not only the bread of life, but the living water that keeps us alive.

Think of that the next time you see beautiful flowers.

Matthew 5:14
"You are the light of the world. A city built on a hill cannot be hid."

Valentine from Heaven

Happy Valentine's Day!

How many of you received a valentine this year from someone you loved? How many did you give to those you love? Valentines are messages we send to let someone know he or she is special and loved.

Can you remember the biggest valentine you have ever gotten? How many times did it say, "You are special and loved"? Did you know you have received a valentine that tells you thousands of times that you are special and loved? Who was it from? You don't know? I'm sure you do, but have not thought of it as a valentine.

The Holy Bible is written to all of us to let us know God loved us so much that He died for us. He did this so that we could have eternal life, if we believe in Him as our Lord and Savior.

Remember this the next time you receive a valentine.

1 John 3:1
See what love the Father has given us, that we should be called the children of God, and that is what we are.

Value

Look at this crisp, clean one-hundred dollar bill. I'm sure all of you would like to have it. It would buy a lot of candy. Watch me as I crumple the bill up, throw it on the floor, stomp on it and get it all greasy and dirty. Now, would you still like to have it? I'm sure you would because all that I did to it did not make it lose its value.

God made us so that we would never lose our value. He accepts us as we are. Our value never changes with God, but Satan tries to make us think we will be rejected by God when our lives get all mixed up and dirty. Don't believe Satan!

The Bible tells us that God made us good and crowned us with honor and glory, and He always accepts us. God made us good even before we were born. Satan can never take our goodness away, because Jesus died for our sins on the cross.

Remember, God made you good the next time you see a bill of money.

Genesis 1:31
God saw everything that he had made, and indeed, it was very good.

Washboard

Have you ever seen one of these before? Can you guess what it is? It's an old washboard that belonged to my mother. My mother and I washed clothes on this board in the spring.

We would boil a pot of water to pour into a tub like this. We would put the clothes in the water to soak for a while and then we would scrub and scrub and scrub, up and down on the tin part of the board. We would then rinse the clothes in clean water and hang them on the line to dry.

I can still remember what Octagon soap smelled like. It smelled so clean. A lot of hard work went into making clothes clean when I was young.

How can we make our hearts clean? The Bible says that the blood of Jesus, shed on the cross, makes us clean. Our faith in Him makes us clean. Sometimes I think Jesus scrubs and scrubs to make us have faith. The Bible says that He can wash us as white as snow.

The next time you smell clean clothes think about Jesus' cleansing power.

Acts 22:16
"And now why do you delay? Get up and be baptized, and have your sins washed away, calling on his name."

Wax

Jesus often taught by giving illustrations or examples. Sometimes the people did not understand what He was trying to teach them. The disciples came and asked Him, "Why do you always use these hard-to-understand illustrations?" Then He explained to them that only they were permitted to understand about the kingdom of heaven, and others were not.

Even the prophet Isaiah said they would hear and not understand. Their hearts would be like this piece of wax. Are our hearts like this piece of wax and don't hear what Jesus is saying to us? If we put a piece of wax in our ears, we do not hear. We have to keep our eyes and ears open to understand what Jesus is saying to us.

We need to read about His teachings and obey them so that our hearts won't become like this piece of wax.

Really pay attention to His teachings and your heart won't become like this piece of wax.

Matthew 13:15
For this people's heart has grown dull, and their ears are hard of hearing, and they have shut their eyes; so that they might not look with their eyes, and listen with their ears, and understand with their heart and turn—and I would heal them.

Weeds

What is this tool I have in my hand? Yes, it is a shovel, but I call it a spade. I use it in my flower garden when I am planting bulbs or getting up grass or weeds. Flower gardens seem to have a lot of grass and weeds.

If I didn't keep the grass out, it would take over the entire flower bed and you could not see the flowers. It is hard to keep out grass and weeds. I sometimes have to get them out everyday to keep a clean flower bed.

The Bible teaches that sin is like grass. It can take over our lives and keep us from being beautiful for God. We have to keep it out at all times. Once we let sin take over, we can do some ugly things. Jesus died on the cross so that our sins could be forgiven.

Try to keep sin out by living for Jesus everyday.

John 3:16
For God so loved the world that he gave his only Son, so that everyone who believes in him may not perish but have eternal life.

Widow's Mite

Let's pretend we are in the synagogue when Jesus was teaching in Jerusalem. Here is a large stone jar used for dropping in your tithes. I will describe the man coming down the aisle . . .

He has on a purple robe and wears a velvet turban around his head. He is walking very slowly as if wanting to be recognized. He has a large money pouch in his hand. It looks like it is full of large coins. When he reaches the altar, he slowly takes a coin out of his pouch, holds it up, looks at it, and then drops it into the jar. The coin makes a loud sound because of its weight. He puts in several other coins that make loud sounds. He looks around to see if anyone has noticed him and slowly walks back down the aisle. He is a rich young ruler.

Here comes someone else down the aisle. Notice how differently she is dressed. She has a large scarf over her head and appears to be poor. She comes to the altar, kneels for a few moments, and puts something into the jar. We can't even hear the coins she drops. She then bows again and leaves very quietly.

The Bible says the rich young ruler gave a large amount. The poor widow gave only two small coins. Jesus said that the widow gave more than all the rich men there put together. They gave only a little of what they owned, but the widow gave all that she had.

Let your offering be from your heart and not for show.

Mark 12:44
"For all of them have contributed out of their abundance; but she out of her poverty has put in everything she had, all she had to live on."

Wind Star

As the wind blows this wooden figure, it changes into different shapes. Watch as the fan blows the figure around. It is fascinating to watch as it changes from one shape to another.

Sometimes we are like the wind star, changing from day to day. We change our minds about things a lot of times. We just go along with the crowd and do what they do.

Jesus wants us to never change our minds about Him, once we have accepted Him into our hearts. Our faith is to remain in Him forever.

God does not change. He takes care of us because He loves us. His love toward us will never change. He promised that He would be with us always. God keeps His promises.

When you see the wind tossing things to and fro, remember that Jesus promised his love for us would never change.

Malachi 3:6
For I the Lord do not change; therefore you, O children of Jacob, have not perished.

Wine Miracle

Here are two jugs of water. Could you turn one jug of water into something else? Maybe if we put some food coloring into one jug, the water would become red. It became red but it did not change the taste of the water at all. It would have been a miracle if it had changed to something else completely.

There was once a wedding in Cana and Jesus was a guest there. The wine had all been drunk and the party was not over. Jesus' mother told Him about the problem. Jesus told a servant to fill up the water pots with water and take some to the master of the party. The master said it was the best wine he had drunk all day long. He said the best wine had been saved until last.

The servants knew immediately what had taken place. This miracle at Cana in Galilee was Jesus' first public demonstration of His heaven-sent power. His disciples believed that He really was the Messiah. He performed many miracles while here on earth.

Read about more miracles in the Bible.

John 2:7
Jesus said to them, "Fill the jars with water." And they filled them up to the brim.

World's Light

This oil lamp is an old lamp that belonged to my mother. When I was young we had no electricity. Can you imagine what life would be like without electricity? We would all sit around the table at night so that we could see to do our homework.

The lamp helped us to see to do many things in the dark. It provided light only when there was oil in the base, the wick had been trimmed, and the globe was clean.

The Bible teaches that Jesus is the light of the world. By learning about Jesus we can learn how to be a light to the world also. He said not to hide our light but to let it shine.

We have to keep our hearts clean in order that our light may shine. We have to keep sin out because sin shuts out light.

Do good deeds so that your light may shine. Thank God for being the light of the world.

Matthew 5:16
"In the same way, let your light shine before others, so that they may see your good works and give glory to your Father in heaven."

Topical Guide

Title	Scripture	Page
Abundance	John 10:10	1
Accountability	Luke 16:10	2
Anchor	Hebrews 6:19	3
Balloons	Luke 6:45	4
Beach Sand	Revelation 1:5	5
Beans & Biscuits	John 3:16	6
Big Eraser	Luke 15:10	7
Boomerang	Luke 6:38	8
Boy Jesus	Luke 2:52	9
Can of Milk	John 14:26	10
Cornerstones	1 Peter 2:6	11
Crayons	John 15:12	12
Crumbs	Matthew 15:27	13
Cups	Matthew 23:25–26	14
David and Goliath	1 Samuel 17:50	15
Direction	John 21:6	16
Dividing Line	Luke 16:25	17
Earth	John 3:16	18
Equipment	John 20:21–22	19
Eye of The Mind	1 Corinthians 3:16	20
Faith and Trust	Hebrews 11:1	21
Fiery Furnace	Daniel 3:28	22
Fishers of Men	Matthew 4:19–20	24
Fishes and Loaves	Luke 9:13	25
Free Gift	Romans 6:23	26
Garden	Genesis 2:8	27
Gideon	Judges 6:16	28
Giving	2 Corinthians 9:6	30

God's Armor	Ephesians 6:11	31
Gold	Psalms 19:10	32
Hearing	Genesis 12:1	33
High Tower	Genesis 11:4	34
Holy Spirit	Acts 2:2	35
How Much Is Enough?	Luke 14:26	36
Living Water	John 4:10	37
Look Inside!	Matthew 7:1	38
Lost and Found	Luke 15:10	39
Love of Money	1 Timothy 6:10	40
Map	John 14:6	41
Millstones	Luke 17:2	42
Mustard Seed	Matthew 17:20	43
Neighbors	Luke 10:36–37	44
New Ground	Luke 10:16	45
Nicodemus	John 3:3	46
Old Shirt	Matthew 25:35–36, 25:40	47
One God	1 John 10:30	48
Oreos and Onions	Matthew 26:39	49
Perfume	John 12:3	50
Persistence	Luke 18:1	51
Peter's Denial	Luke 22:34	52
Plow	Luke 9:62	53
Potter's Clay	Jeremiah 18:5–6	54
Prayer	Matthew 6:9–13	55
Prodigal Son	Luke 15:20	56
Race	Hebrews 12:1–2	57
Rainbow	Genesis 9:13	58
Rubies	Proverbs 3:15	60
Smell the Bread	Matthew 26:26	61
Sower	Matthew 13:1–3	62
Special Apples	1 John 3:1	64
Sponges	John 15:8	65

Stones	Luke 19:40	66
Ten Commandments	Deuteronomy 5:22	67
Thorns	Matthew 27:29	70
Time	Ecclesiastes 3:1	71
Title	2 Corinthians 1:21-22	72
Transformation	2 Corinthians 5:17	73
Treasure Box	Luke 12:34	74
True Vine	John 15:1	75
Two Flower Baskets	Matthew 5:14	76
Valentine from Heaven	1 John 3:1	77
Value	Genesis 1:31	78
Washboard	Acts 22:16	79
Wax	Matthew 13:15	80
Weeds	John 3:16	81
Widow's Mite	Mark 12:44	82
Wind Star	Malachi 3:6	83
Wine Miracle	John 2:7	84
World's Light	Matthew 5:16	85

Scriptural Guide

Scripture	Title	Page
Acts 2:2	Holy Spirit	35
Acts 22:16	Washboard	79
1 Corinthians 3:16	Eye of the Mind	20
2 Corinthians 1:21-22	Title	72
2 Corinthians 5:17	Transformation	73
2 Corinthians 9:6	Giving	30
Daniel 3:28	Fiery Furnace	22
Deuteronomy 5:22	Ten Commandments	67
Ecclesiastes 3:1	Time	71
Ephesians 6:11	God's Armor	31
Genesis 2:8	Garden	27
Genesis 1:31	Value	78
Genesis 9:13	Rainbow	58
Genesis 11:4	High Tower	34
Genesis 12:1	Hearing	33
Hebrews 6:19	Anchor	3
Hebrews 11:1	Faith and Trust	21
Hebrews 12:1–2	Race	57
Jeremiah 18:5–6	Potter's Clay	54
1 John 3:1	Special Apples	64
1 John 3:1	Valentine from Heaven	77
1 John 10:30	One God	48
John 2:7	Wine Miracle	84
John 3:3	Nicodemus	46
John 3:16	Beans and Biscuits	6
John 3:16	Earth	18
John 3:16	Weeds	81
John 4:10	Living Water	37

Reference	Title	Page
John 10:10	Abundance	1
John 12:3	Perfume	50
John 14:6	Map	41
John 14:26	Can of Milk	10
John 15:1	True Vine	75
John 15:8	Sponges	65
John 15:12	Crayons	12
John 20:21–22	Equipment	19
John 21:6	Direction	16
Judges 6:16	Gideon	28
Luke 2:52	Boy Jesus	9
Luke 6:38	Boomerang	8
Luke 6:45	Balloons	4
Luke 9:13	Fishes and Loaves	25
Luke 9:62	Plow	53
Luke 10:16	New Ground	45
Luke 10:36–37	Neighbors	44
Luke 12:34	Treasure Box	74
Luke 14:26	How Much Is Enough?	36
Luke 15:10	Big Eraser	7
Luke 15:10	Lost and Found	39
Luke 15:20	Prodigal Son	56
Luke 16:10	Accountability	2
Luke 16:25	Dividing Line	17
Luke 17:2	Millstones	42
Luke 18:1	Persistence	51
Luke 19:40	Stones	66
Luke 22:34	Peter's Denial	52
Malachi 3:6	Wind Star	83
Mark 12:44	Widow's Mite	82
Matthew 4:19–20	Fishers of Men	24
Matthew 5:14	Two Flower Baskets	76
Matthew 5:16	World's Light	85

Matthew 6:9–13	Prayer	55
Matthew 7:1	Look Inside!	38
Matthew 13:1–3	Sower	62
Matthew 13:15	Wax	80
Matthew 15:27	Crumbs	13
Matthew 17:20	Mustard Seed	43
Matthew 23:25–26	Cups	14
Matthew 25:35–36, 25:40	Old Shirt	47
Matthew 26:26	Smell The Bread	61
Matthew 26:39	Oreos and Onions	49
Matthew 27:29	Thorns	70
1 Peter 2:6	Cornerstones	11
Proverbs 3:15	Rubies	60
Psalms 19:10	Gold	32
Revelation 1:5	Beach Sand	5
Romans 6:23	Free Gift	26
1 Samuel 17:50	David and Goliath	15
1 Timothy 6:10	Love of Money	40